Bright Ideas
Dance and Movement

Written by Kate Harrison, Jane Layton
and Melanie Morris

Published by Scholastic Publications Ltd,
Marlborough House, Holly Walk,
Leamington Spa, Warwickshire CV32 4LS.

© 1989 Scholastic Publications Ltd

Written by Kate Harrison, Jane Layton and
Melanie Morris
Edited by Christine Lee
Sub-edited by Julie Smart and Jane Morgan
Illustrations by Jane Andrews
Artwork by Liz Preece,
Castle Graphics, Kenilworth.

Printed in Great Britain by
Loxley Brothers Ltd, Sheffield

British Library Cataloguing in Publication Data
Bright Ideas.
  Dance & Movement.
  1. Primary schools. Activities.
  I. Harrison, Kate II. Morris, Melanie III. Layton,
  Jane
  372.19

ISBN 0-590-76014-9

Front and back cover: designed by Sue Limb;
illustration by Jane Andrews.

Contents

Introduction

Dance in education develops children's ability to communicate through a non-verbal language, a body language, a language without words.

Education gives children vocabularies with which to investigate life and to articulate their findings. Dance has its own vocabulary. This vocabulary can be divided into four areas.

ACTION: WHAT CAN I DO?
- Transferring weight: step, sit, kneel, rock, sway, flop, collapse, fall, handstand, cartwheel.
- Jumping: hop, leap, bounce.
- Travelling: run, roll, slither, creep.
- Turning: spin, spiral, twirl, twist.
- Gesturing: stretch, reach, balance, wave, kick, nod, clap, pull, push, grab, hug, lean, slap.

SPACE: WHERE DO I DO IT?
- Direction: forwards, backwards, sideways, straight, curved, zig-zag, up, down, across, over, under, through, near, far, towards, away from, surround.
- Size: big, small.
- Shape: curved, twisted, pointed.

DYNAMICS: HOW DO I DO IT?
Quickly, slowly, powerfully, gently, directly, sharply, floppily, alertly, lazily.

RELATIONSHIP: WITH WHOM DO I DO IT?

Approach, meet, part, pass, with, against, lead, follow, question, answer, together, separately, alone, me, my partner, a group.

These are, of course, only a few examples. We can train children to increase their skills in all these areas, but dancing is more than just a compilation of skilful movements. Making dances involves the selection of the appropriate movement vocabulary in order to investigate, express or communicate a particular idea or image.

This book demonstrates this process over and over again in a concise form. Each activity defines the image or idea in bold type and then gives suggested movement material. The activities are not intended as single lessons; indeed, most contain enough material for several lessons, even half a term's work. Nor is the material necessarily to be used sequentially. The activities are not lists or sequences of things to do, to be followed in a 'recipe' fashion. The idea is to select two to four of the images to form a lesson.

The activities are grouped into chapters, and at the beginning of each chapter there is a diagram showing the contents. If the title of the chapter is the topic you are using with your class (eg Weather) some or all of the material in the section will be useful. Alternatively, links between chapters can be made. For example, if you have used 'Superpeople' (from Flight) you could then investigate the disaster area to which

Superperson is flying, eg 'Burning buildings' (from Fire and light). From each chapter, or each chart, select as much or as little as your class topic or curriculum work needs.

Some class topics will need to use material from several sections. A topic on 'Water' might use material from 'Rain rhymes 1' (from Weather), 'Icebergs' (from Where in the world?) and 'Life in the pond' (from Mini-beasts). A project based on the

Chinese New Year might use material from 'Kites' (from Flight), 'Dragon monsters' (from Magic, mystery and monsters), 'Fireworks' (from Fire and light) and 'The Emperor and the Nightingale' (from Animals). A project based on a legend, for example the Ramayana from India, might use material from the chapters on Weather, Where in the world?, Animals and Fire and light.

It is important that the imagery is used in a sensitive way. It should not only encourage the movement content desired, but be accessible and reflect the needs, experience and culture of the children involved. The text is sensitive to the different sorts of experiences which children have, be they first-hand experiences such as 'Weather' and 'Out and about', or second-hand (removed) experiences such as reading about something, copying a picture from a book or fantasy and imaginary experiences. All experiences, be they everyday, frequent or occasional, can be valuable starting points for creative dance work.

These experiences vary according to the personal, social, religious or cultural calendars of the teacher and the child. For example, in 'Picnic basket' (from Picnics and parties) crunchy crisps are suggested to encourage sharp shapes and quick jumps. However, some picnic baskets might contain other crispy foods, such as poppadams or prawn crackers. Similarly, throughout the world there are stories told about huge beasts which frighten people but which are eventually overcome. An example of this is the 'Dragon monster' (from Magic, mystery and monsters).

The aim is to allow the user maximum flexibility within a clearly defined structure. We recognise that the text may, on first reading, appear to be prescriptive. But this format has evolved over many years in response to recurring requests from teachers. It works! It gives teachers the opportunity to select as much or as little material as they need, and thus confidently to continue to teach dance creatively week by week throughout the school year. Therefore both pupil and teacher alike learn by doing. Together they are involved in a process of 'doing, making and looking'. Together, no matter how simple or complex the movement material may be, they are involved in the art of making dances.

Eventually we hope that you will find your own image or idea and select the appropriate movement content. This book is all about bright ideas and is intended as a starting, not a finishing, point for teachers and children.

THE TEACHER'S ROLE EVALUATION!

You as the teacher are the link between the text and the children and, as you know, all children are very sensitive to the attitude and involvement of their teacher. You alone can see how well the children understand and perform each activity and to what extent it needs to be practised further. Only

you can praise, encourage and comment on the quality of the children's actions. Be an active participant, not a passive observer. This does not necessarily mean doing the actions yourself, but making sure that the children give of their very best. The quest for quality is more easily seen than defined in words. It is achieving something never done before, or doing it better than before. Quality is relative to the age and experience of the child, but it is always demanding and almost never fully achieving.

ORGANISATION
BEFORE THE LESSON
To get the best out of the text you need to prepare by:
● Providing a hall or a large space suitable for movement activities.
● Ensuring that the children are suitably dressed, ie vests and pants, PE kit or 'dance gear'. Bare feet are preferable, but if the floor is old and/or dirty, soft shoes should be worn.
● Collecting a few percussion instruments, eg drum, tambourine, bells and woodblocks, for your own use during the lesson.
● Selecting a suitable musical accompaniment if necessary. Good, simple well-constructed sounds and music can be used to stimulate and accompany movement activities. However, music is not essential to the successful development of creative movement, so allow plenty of time for exploration and practice without any sound or musical accompaniment.

DURING THE LESSON

- Observe and comment on children's responses.
- Repeat an activity if you are not satisfied with the children's work.
- Always be aware of spacing and use your initiative to prevent the children bunching together.
- Ensure that the children start and stop on cue.
- Ask for new ideas from the children.
- Value the responses the children make to the images they are given.
- Always be on the look-out for children who need help and those whom you can choose to demonstrate an activity for the others to observe. Observation helps them to compare and contrast their efforts and to raise their standards of achievement. Look for those who have improved on their own personal standard, and avoid selecting the same children each time.

AFTER THE LESSON

The ideas and images in the activities can be used as springboards for other activities, as outlined earlier in this introduction.

This book gives you at least 500 bright ideas for dance. Don't be afraid to have some more bright ideas of your own.

Kate Harrison
Jane Layton
Melanie Morris

Weather

The weather is part of a child's daily life and provides immediate experience from which valuable creative movement activities can be generated.

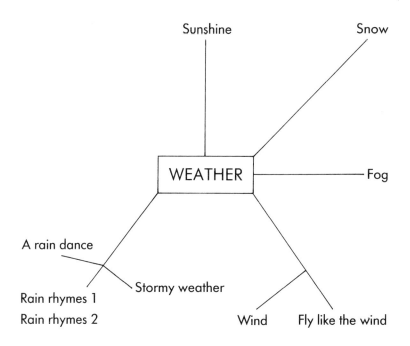

Sunshine   Snow

WEATHER — Fog

A rain dance

Rain rhymes 1
Rain rhymes 2   Stormy weather

Wind   Fly like the wind

Sunshine

Age range
Five to eleven.

Emphasis
Skipping skills as individuals and in pairs, in lines and in circles.

We're happy because the sun is shining, so let's make a skipping dance.

Skip:
- Individually, in and out of spaces, forwards, backwards and sideways.
- In pairs, in and out of spaces, leading and following, holding hands, forwards, backwards and sideways.
- In a class line, changing leaders on command, the leader skips to the back of the line, leaving a new leader to carry on.

- In several group lines, taking care not to skip through another line.
- In a class circle, round one way, round the other way, into the centre and out again.
- In a class circle, with one person skipping round the circle and back to the starting place while the others clap.

- Standing in spaces, with one leader skipping in and out of the others. The leader taps each person gently on the shoulder and they join on behind to form a skipping line.

Repeat this with several leaders starting at the same time. Incorporate clapping while skipping, clapping in front of the tummy, behind the back, above the head or under the knees.

Snow

Age range
Five to nine.

Emphasis
Contrasting light with heavy, and big with small.

Tiny snowflakes flutter and fall.
Start in a space with arms stretched up high and flutter fingers lightly and gently, arms sinking slowly around the body.

Soft fluffy snowflakes fall.
Take light quick hops, jumps, leaps and turns from space to space with arms outstretched.
Fast fluttering flakes turn into a swirling snowstorm.
Practise fast smooth turning, high and low, with pauses before changing direction. Stress keeping arms outstretched on turns, circling around the body on pauses. Encourage jumping and turning then balances on pauses.

You've made a snowman!
From a curled shape on the floor, grow slowly and strongly upwards into a big wide shape standing with feet apart and arms outstretched.
The sun has come out!
Start from a big, wide stretched shape and sink one body part at a time to the floor, slowly and smoothly, until the whole body is lying flat on the floor in a 'puddle' shape.

A carpet of snow.
Start from a stretched shape standing up, then slowly and smoothly sink to the floor making wide, stretched 'snow crystal' shapes, on tummies or backs, with limbs outstretched. Join on to another snow crystal shape nearby with fingers and toes.
Trudging through deep snow.
Encourage big heavy steps forwards, backwards, sideways and round and round, arms outstretched to help balance.
Rolling snowballs in deep snow.
Start curled up in a tight ball on the floor in a space then, keeping the shape, roll slowly, smoothly and strongly forwards, backwards, sideways and round and round.

Fog

Age range
Five to eleven.

Emphasis
Directions: forwards, backwards and sideways.

It's so foggy, you can't see where you're going.
Take long, low slow steps, sometimes forwards, sometimes backwards and sometimes sideways, pausing to change direction, individually or with a partner.

It's so foggy, you can't see where anything is. A cat brushes past the back of your legs. Ugh!
Step as above, then make a sudden jump forwards.
A gate swings open into your hip. Ouch!
Stepping as above, but make a sudden jump sideways.
Who put that lamp-post there? A bicycle zooms past. Whoops!
Stepping as above, make a sudden jump backwards then a fast turn, using arms to help.
What is that sound and where is it coming from?
Stand with one hand behind an ear, head leading sideways, stretching slowly into a wide balance, then stretch slowly into different balancing shapes, head leading forwards, backwards, up or down.

Fly like the wind

Go wind, blow
Push wind, swoosh
Shake things,
Take things,
Make things fly.
Ring things,
Swing things,
Fling things high.
Go wind, blow
Push things . . . wheee
No, wind, no
   Not me —
    not *me*.

Lilian Moore

Age range
Seven to eleven.

Emphasis
Using the words 'go', 'blow', 'push', 'swoosh', 'shake', 'fly', 'ring', 'swing', 'fling' and 'wheee' to initiate contrasting dynamics.

Go wind, blow.
Run in many directions, then freeze.
Push wind, swoosh.
Push forward with hands, then run to a new space.
Shake things,
Take things,
Make things fly.
Shake the whole body, hands, fingers and head.
Contrast this with gliding from high to low.

Ring things,
Swing things,
Fling things high.
Make turning, whirling actions leading to leaps in the air.
Go wind, blow.
Push things . . . wheee.
Repeat the first two sections, then shout 'Wheee!' while swooping from high to low levels.
No, wind, no.
Not me – not *me*.
Turn round and round, closing up from a wide body shape into a tight ball.

Wind

Age range
Five to eleven.

Emphasis
Moving and stopping in a variety of ways.

Small gusts of wind.
Start with knees slightly bent, back curved over forwards and arms rounded, then quickly and gently lift the head or stretch an arm or leg out into the space before slowly and gently returning to the starting shape. Use these ideas, starting from a rounded shape on knees or on backs, pausing between each one and allowing a slow recovery of the head, arms or legs, to change into a new shape, such as from standing to knees.

Whirlwind.
Spiral quickly upwards on to tiptoes with arms lifted, then spiral downwards the other way, lowering the arms. Spiral upwards and downwards, travelling from space to space, pausing before spiralling upwards again.

Hurricane.
Combine the whirlwind movements with strong high leaps and jumps.

Whirlwinds and hurricanes bend young trees . . .
Stand on both feet, knees bent, arms stretching to the front, the back or to the side. Bend slowly from the waist forwards, backwards and sideways as far as possible while maintaining balance. Bend from the waist, making a stretched shape supported on one foot.

. . . and even big old trees with deep roots.
Make wide group shapes joined at the hips, backs or shoulders, stretching as many arms and legs out into the space as possible. Everyone sways and bends as far as possible in different directions, remaining joined together.

Trees crack and splinter.
Working individually or in a group shape, quickly and strongly 'snap' arms downwards, while stamping feet and lunging along the floor.

Whirlwinds and hurricanes bend tall buildings . . .
Make tall group shapes standing on tiptoes reaching one or both arms upwards, or balancing on shoulders, reaching legs and feet upwards. Sway and bend as far as possible in different directions.

. . . which eventually crumble.
From a tall group shape, drop, crouch or curl quickly one at a time to the floor, before slowly rolling away from the group.

The wind creates havoc in the street. Dustbin lids roll.
Roll, sometimes quickly, sometimes slowly. Cartwheel slowly and smoothly, concentrating on the roundness of the action.

Boxes bounce and balance.
In a wide flat shape, or a shape with a clear right angle at the hips, jump sharply from one foot to the other, sometimes turning, sometimes pausing in a clear balance. Cartwheel quickly and jerkily, concentrating on the sharpness of the action, holding a clear shape between each cartwheel.

Gates swing open and bang shut.
Work in pairs, standing tall with one arm reaching upwards. Stretch one arm or leg forwards or sideways to join with the partner to make a 'gate'. Slowly open the 'gate', turning as far as possible. Then quickly close the 'gate' to join up again.

The power of the wind.
Combine all the above ideas. Some children can explore the way the wind moves, while others experiment with the different effects on trees, buildings and gates.

A rain dance

Age range
Five to eleven.

Emphasis
Using percussion instruments to initiate and accompany dance.

The land is dry – it has not rained for months. A raindrop falls to earth – plip-plop.
Play random notes on a xylophone and encourage sudden, light spiky changes of shape using knees, elbows, fingers and heads to represent raindrops.
The raindrops fall one after another; faster and faster they swirl around.
Jump around the room, still in spiky body shapes.

Gradually change these movements into continuous running, using curved arm gestures, whirling at high and low levels.

The raindrops form small puddles on the muddy ground.
At the gentle stroke of a cymbal, run towards each other to form groups of five or six. Each group meets close together in a low shape.

The puddles grow and grow.
Stretch slowly outwards, accompanied by a gentle roll on the cymbal.

Suddenly the water breaks away and flows in all directions.
Make crashing noises with the cymbal, followed by maracas shaking. The groups break away with individuals running and pausing into spaces.

The land is covered with streams. These join together to form a river which gushes through the earth.
Lead the class in one long line. Work on winding pathways, pushing with arms rising and sinking as you run. Practise this individually first.

Rain rhymes 1

Rain, rain, go away
Come again another day.

Age range
Three to seven.

Emphasis
Simple, rhythmic whole-body activities on the spot, from space to space and round the room.

Start with the children seated round you and chant the rhyme through several times. Then clap the rhythm of the words and stamp it out, either sitting with feet beating the floor or standing stamping on the spot. Develop these activities by encouraging the children to stamp and clap in and out of the spaces in the room while chanting the rhyme.

23

When everyone has mastered this slow, strong stamping and clapping rhythm, divide them into two groups. One group stamps and chants, 'Rain, rain, go away', the other replies, 'Come again another day'. Use the words 'go away' and 'come again' to introduce moving forwards and backwards. Find other ways of moving to this rhythm – jumping, hopping, skipping or galloping.

Rain rhymes 2

Pitter, patter, pitter, patter,
Listen to the rain.
Pitter, patter, pitter, patter,
On the window pane.

Age range
Three to seven.

Emphasis
Lightness and strength.

Contrast the strong, rhythmic stamping steps of 'Rain, rain, go away' with fingertips tapping lightly on the floor in time to the quick, whispery words. Then run quickly and quietly from space to space, whispering the words of the rhyme. Introduce statue stops at the end of each line and use these to check the spacing and lightness of movement.

There are many other traditional rain rhymes, such as 'It's raining, it's pouring' and 'Dr Foster went to Gloucester' which can be used in this way.

Stormy weather

Age range
Five to eleven.

Emphasis
Using the words 'roll', 'flash', 'blow', 'cluster', 'burst' and 'reach' to stimulate strong contrasting actions.

The thunder rolls!
Roll along the ground from high to low levels.
Lightning flashes!
Jump jerkily and shoot out arms and fingers at high and low levels in short, staccato phrases.

The wind blows!
Make whirling, swirling, rushing and pushing movements.
Clouds cluster.
Gather together and form a huge class cloud shape, then rise up high together.
A cloudburst.
Jump and dart, run and stop in and out of spaces to represent the rain dispersing from the cloud to the land.
A rainbow reaches across the sky.
Make a slow growing and spreading action individually, in pairs or as a class group, to represent an arched 'rainbow' shape.

Where in the world?

This chapter considers different climates and terrains as starting points for dance.

The ideas of journeying through jungle, across desert, through swamps, over snowy mountain peaks and along ridges are achieved through a variety of appropriate and contrasting actions.

Huge leaves uncurl and spread out over the jungle.
Start curled up small in a space then grow upwards on both feet, slowly and strongly, reaching out into a wide, stretched balanced shape on one foot. Try balances which stretch forwards or sideways.

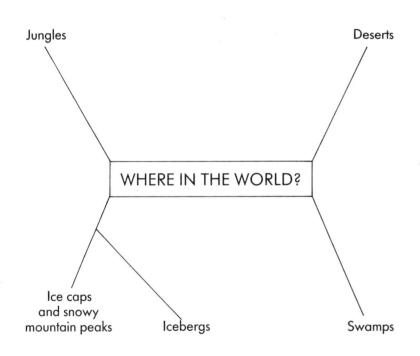

Jungles

Deserts

WHERE IN THE WORLD?

Ice caps
and snowy
mountain peaks

Icebergs

Swamps

Jungles

Age range
Five to eleven.

Emphasis
Over, under, around and through a variety of group shapes.

The giant leaves, scorched by the sun, shrivel and die.
Stretch into a balance then tip off balance and pull arms
and legs quickly into a tuck position. Land carefully on
the floor and roll quickly over and over in a ball to a new
space.

**New leaves stretch and unfold; old leaves die and rot on
the forest floor.**
Put the whole movement sequence together. Start curled
up; grow slowly into a wide, stretched balanced shape;
tip off balance; carefully fall and roll in a ball shape to
a new space and begin the sequence again.

Develop this by starting sequences at different times,
so that wide stretched balances are growing and tipping
over the top of rolling shapes.

28

Tangled shapes in the undergrowth.

Curl up small in groups of three then grow into wide stretched shapes. Encourage lots of gaps between limbs. Develop the shapes into balances then get the children to roll over together to a new space.

Explorers move over, under, around and through the undergrowth.

Divide the class in half then ask them to form groups of three. One half grows into tangled undergrowth shapes together; the other creeps carefully over, under and around the different tangled undergrowth shapes.

Change over so that everyone has a chance to practise all the activities.

How can we get through the deep dark undergrowth?

Slither and slide slowly and strongly on stomachs, sides and backs. Make slow, careful backward rolls.

How can we get over the thorny bushes?

Take slow, careful stretched steps lifting legs high; light stretched leaps using arms to help balance; and light high hops, forwards, sideways and backwards.

How can we get around the tall, dark tree trunks?

Take slow, careful creeping steps along winding pathways; sometimes making full circles before changing direction.

Deserts

Age range
Five to eleven.

Emphasis
Using the texture of sand to stimulate stepping, balancing and rolling.

Walking on burning hot sand.
Take quick, light sharp steps, pulling feet up off the floor with knees high. Move forwards, backwards, sideways and round and round with light quick jumps and hops.

Wading through sand.
Take slow heavy steps using arms to help balance.

Rolling down a sand dune . . . splash into an oasis!
Roll in small curled or long thin shapes across the floor, then make one big jump into or out of the 'oasis'.

Develop this in pairs so that one person rolls fast while the other takes slow, strong wading steps. The pairs then join wrists and the wader helps the other person out of the oasis. Finish with one huge jump then change roles.

Swamps

Age range
Seven to ten.

Emphasis
Using the texture of swamps to stimulate jumping, turning and stepping.

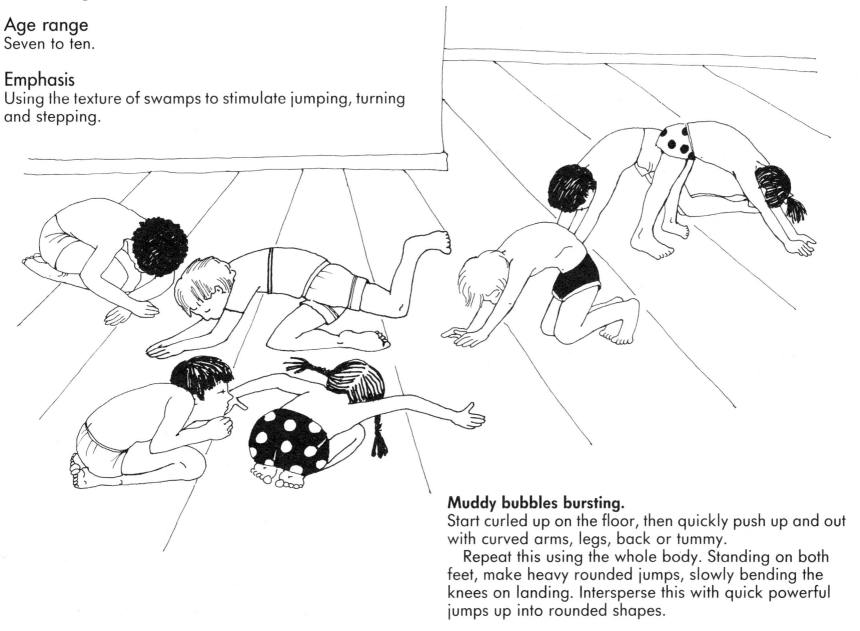

Muddy bubbles bursting.
Start curled up on the floor, then quickly push up and out with curved arms, legs, back or tummy.

Repeat this using the whole body. Standing on both feet, make heavy rounded jumps, slowly bending the knees on landing. Intersperse this with quick powerful jumps up into rounded shapes.

Ice caps and snowy mountain peaks

Age range
Five to nine.

Emphasis
Travelling along, balancing on, jumping across and hiding behind.

Crossing a ridge.
Tiptoe slowly and carefully along a straight line, one foot directly in front of the other, using arms to help balance.

Slow spiralling steam.
Turn slowly and smoothly, spiralling up and down from space to space. Make sure that the children spiral one way, pause, then spiral the other way to stop them feeling dizzy.

Wading through the swamp. I'm stuck! Help!
Take long dragging steps then one body part becomes stuck. Ask the children to demonstrate which part is stuck: a leg? an arm? the back? Encourage them to pull and tug, trying to free the part that is stuck.

A knife-edge ridge.
Move as above, but with pauses holding clear balancing shapes on one or both feet.
Jumping from iceberg to iceberg. Be careful not to fall in the ice-cold sea!
Make light careful jumps, hops, leaps and balances, landing on one or both feet. Turn to face different directions after each balancing action.

Quick – hide! Hide from the polar bear!
Run with quick light steps in and out of spaces. Freeze on the command 'Hide!'.
Hide behind a small craggy rock.
Sink to a small round shape and hold very still. Repeat running and stopping on command.
Hide behind a stalagmite.
Stretch up tall, long and thin on tiptoe with arms reaching upwards. Repeat the running and stopping on command.

Icebergs

Age range
Five to eleven.

Emphasis
Growing and shrinking, slowly and suddenly.

Sharp jagged icebergs jutting out of the sea.
Curl up then grow slowly and strongly upwards into sharp angular shapes with bent elbows and knees or long extended shapes with stretched arms, legs and

Nowhere to hide. Quick! Lie flat on an iceberg!
Lie flat and wide on the floor.
Where will you choose to hide this time? Behind a small craggy rock? Or a stalagmite?
Repeat the running and stopping sequence, allowing a choice of one of the hiding shapes on each statue stop. Encourage clear, still body shapes with only eyes moving to see where the others are hiding.

fingers. Incorporate balances forwards or sideways.

Icebergs shatter, splinter and break.
Make sharp, jerky percussive actions with arms, legs, backs and heads, making definite pauses before stepping and sinking to a new space.

Icebergs dripping, melting in the sun.
Grow from low curled shapes into sharp spiky shapes, holding balances.

Which part of the iceberg is going to melt first? The tip? One side? The bottom?
Move one body part at a time slowly and smoothly towards the floor, starting with the head, arms, back or one leg, until all hang limp and flop to the floor.

Huge towering icebergs.
In groups of three, grow into sharp, jagged spiky shapes and balances at different levels.

Picnics and parties

Picnics, parties and party food provide some fun starting points for a variety of movement activities and dancing games.

There are themes for the very young such as 'The Teddy Bears' Picnic'. Older children will enjoy creating a class forest and then playing a game of hide and seek. Alternatively, they could have an imaginary class picnic or party and play musical statues, circle and follow-my-leader games.

Food themes include cooking with eggs, tossing pancakes and there is a host of surprises inside the picnic basket.

Just enjoy yourselves! That's what party time is all about!

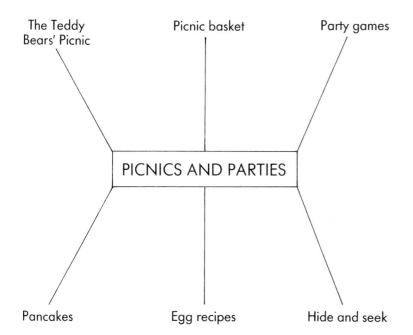

The Teddy Bears' Picnic

Age range
Three to seven.

Emphasis
Using a popular children's song as a stimulus for a variety of activities.

Start with the children standing around you, singing the song and clapping together. Then ask them to skip away from you with heads held high and high knees.
Big bears.
Push upwards and outwards with round fists from curled shapes to wide, stretched shapes.
Bouncing bears.
Jump into wide shapes with feet apart.

Little bears.
Run quickly and quietly on hands and feet from space to space, making occasional statue stops.
Naughty bears.
Run and stop at high and low levels as though playing 'hide and seek'.
Playing together.
In pairs, clasp hands and dance round and round on the spot. In pairs, hold one hand and skip together around the edge of the room. Stand one behind the other and march from space to space with frequent statue stops and changes in direction.
Performing bears balancing on a tightrope.
Balance with one foot in the air, then on hands and feet, then hands and knees, with one or two limbs in the air.

Step carefully along a straight pathway with statue stops and a variety of balances.
Acrobatic bears.
Jump, leap, roll and balance. Encourage individual interpretation but emphasise the need for safety.

The Teddy Bears' Picnic:
Lots of honey.
Pull 'sticky' hands and feet slowly away from the floor.
Wobbly jellies.
Shake, wiggle and wobble from high to low.
A big round cake.
Stretch slowly and spread out to the edge of the room so that everyone is standing in a circle.

Picnic basket

Age range
Four to seven.

Emphasis
Shapes; different ways of travelling.

Out crackle the crunchy crisps!
On a given signal, change quickly from a strong shape with bent arms and legs to a stiff spiky shape. Jump or turn quickly from one 'crunchy' shape to another.
Out roll some snappy Twiglets!
Start from an upright position or lie straight on the floor, then turn or roll in long, thin stretched shapes, pausing to reach away from the body with arms and legs.

Dancing bears:
A skipping circle.
Be ready to indicate the direction of travel and insist on no overtaking.
A marching line.
Choose one child as a leader (or lead yourself) to take the children out of the circle with high marching steps to form one long line.
Tired little teddy bears.
Travel with slow heavy steps, one behind the other round the edge of the room.
Tiptoeing together.
Take big, slow silent steps to form a class group then sink together to the floor.

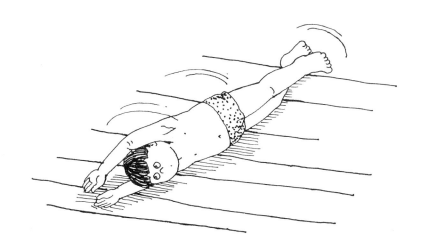

tops; pineapples with bumps and tufts. Make a fruit cocktail shape in a group.

Stick in a wafer.
One person jumps quickly into the group shape, making either a long thin or wide flat wafer shape.

Pour on the cream.
One person carefully runs, jumps and slithers through the group 'fruit cocktail' shape.

Hot, sticky chocolate biscuits.
Stand facing each other in pairs in wide stretched shapes. Mirror each other, carefully and slowly sinking to the floor, using one body part at a time.

Who fancies a fruit cocktail? What fruits did you put in yours?
Make different fruit shapes: long thin bananas; round apples; mangoes and pears with fat bottoms and thin

Party games

Age range
Five to eleven.

Emphasis
Starting and stopping, follow-my-leader and circle formations.

Musical statues.
Play 'musical statues' using different travelling actions and a variety of body shapes. Establish moving when the music plays and stopping as soon as the music stops. Listen before moving to check whether the sounds are quick or slow. Play animal and fancy dress statues with the children moving and stopping as the shape of a chosen animal or character.

Grandmother's footsteps/What's the time Mr Wolf?
Stand at one end of the room with the children spaced out at the other end. Progress from slow tiptoeing to running on tiptoes with silent steps and clear statue stops.

Follow my leader.
Use the follow-my-leader formation to teach basic travelling activities such as jumping, hopping, skipping, galloping, trotting, jogging, striding and marching. Play

or clap the rhythm and change leaders so that all the children have a chance to lead the lines. For a more humorous version, each new leader must find a funny way of walking.

Lines and circles.

Organise the class into two lines. Ask them to march, following the leader, up and down the room along straight pathways. Change the leaders and ask the lines

to skip round the room to make one or two circles. The circles could then skip in clockwise and anti-clockwise directions. When sufficient spatial awareness is displayed, the children can make one long class follow-my-leader line and travel along figure-of-eight pathways.

'Here we go round the mulberry bush, the mulberry bush, the mulberry bush!
Here we go round the mulberry bush on a cold and frosty morning!'
Practise forming a class circle quickly and quietly with and without holding hands. Stand in the centre of the circle then indicate the direction in which the children should travel. Ask for skipping with heads held high, high knees and no overtaking.
'This is the way we stretch up tall, stretch up tall, stretch up tall!'

Make sure that the children are well spaced in a circle before starting these isolated body actions.
'This is the way we curl down small on a cold and frosty morning.'
Let the children develop this game by choosing a variety of 'on the spot' and 'travelling' actions for themselves, for example jumping, hopping, clapping, trotting and galloping.
'Here we go round . . . This is the way we . . .'
Encourage the children to suggest new activities and ask them to demonstrate their choice to the others.

43

Hide and seek

Age range
Five to eleven.

Emphasis
Starting and stopping; making different shapes.

1, 2, 3 . . . The counting has begun.
Take small, quick, light running steps from space to
space, pausing to change direction.
50, 51, 52 . . . Is anyone coming to search yet? 99, 100

. . . Quick! Where can I hide?
Run and pause to look behind, peering between legs,
turning on tiptoes or twisting around.

Behind a tree stump?
Curl into small round shapes on or near the floor.

Behind a tree?
Stretch into tall thin shapes on tiptoes, with arms and fingers stretched above the head.

Under the autumn leaves?
Stretch into wide flat shapes on the floor.

So many good hiding places; it's difficult to choose.
Run with small, quick light steps from space to space, stopping quickly in different 'hiding' shapes, before running again.

No room for two! If someone borrows your hiding place go and find another.
Divide the class into two with one half stretching tall, curling small or lying flat, the other half running quickly in and out of the hiding shapes. Ask the ones running about to choose someone who is making a clear hiding shape, then copy this shape in front of, behind, or to the side of the hiding person. The hiding person must run quickly to find another person in a clear hiding shape.

Sardines.
Form hiding shapes by stretching, curling or lying down. Choose several class leaders to run quickly in and out of the hiding shapes and let them choose someone to hide with, copying their hiding shape and pausing together. Then, together, they run quickly to choose a third person to hide with, copying their hiding shape, pausing together, before running to find another person, and so on. Continue until the whole class is involved.

Egg recipes

Age range
Seven to eleven.

Emphasis
Using the words 'roll', 'crack', 'ooze', 'bubble', 'squeak', 'flip', 'whisk' and 'scramble' to stimulate different shapes and dynamics.

Eggs roll.
Form a small round shape, rolling slowly in one direction and then another.

Eggs crack.
Make sharp jagged shapes, using bent fingers, wrists, elbows, shoulders, hips, knees, ankles and toes, standing on both feet, then balancing on one foot. Encourage changing quickly and powerfully from one jagged shape to another.

Eggs ooze.
Start from a jagged broken shape, then stretch the whole body, slowly and smoothly into a 'fried egg' shape.

Fried eggs bubble and squeak.
Start in a big, stretched 'fried egg' shape on the floor, on tummy or back. Shoot an arm or a leg high into the air and back again.

Fried egg flip.
Change slowly and carefully from 'fried egg' shapes on backs to 'fried egg' shapes on tummies by rolling sideways, stretching arms and legs towards the ceiling while turning over.

Sunny side up.
Start in a 'fried egg' shape and quickly lift bottom towards the ceiling to balance on hands and feet, then slowly 'ooze' on to the floor again.

Whisking whites.
Jump quickly and lightly from one foot to the other, turning in the air with arms outstretched and knees tucked up, landing softly.

Scrambling yolks.
Run very quickly on the spot, wriggling every part of the body quickly and jerkily. Wriggle the whole body while rising and sinking, turning from one place to another, pausing to change direction.

Pancakes

Age range
Five to eleven.

Emphasis
Starting and stopping with changes in level.

It's time to make pancakes!
Run carefully with knees slightly bent, one arm outstretched, along twisting pathways.
It's time to toss the pancakes high into the air and catch them!
Run quickly along twisting pathways. Incorporate turning on the spot, quickly and powerfully, lifting one arm high in the air and looking upwards.
Oops! You've dropped the pancakes. Where did they land?
Crawl, slowly and carefully, along the floor, forwards, backwards and sideways.
Oops! The pancakes are stuck on the ceiling. Can you reach them?
Make big, powerful, bouncing jumps on the spot, reaching and looking upwards.

For older children, tossing the pancake could involve a turning jump. Catching the pancake might involve rolling.

Animals

Animals never fail to fascinate the very young and even the most sophisticated eleven-year-olds will happily investigate the movement potential of their favourite pet or wild creature.

This chapter covers a variety of animals, ranging from the farmyard to the zoo, from nursery rhymes to traditional stories. The choice is yours. All the given activities can be adapted to other animal themes and stories.

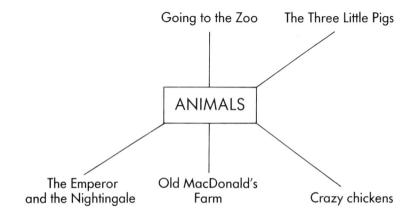

Going to the Zoo

Age range
Three to eleven.

Emphasis
Using recorded music to initiate and accompany dance. 'Going to the Zoo' can be found on *Amazing Grace*, Julie Felix (Meteor).

Sit and sing the song while clapping the beat. Skip lightly around the room. Find different ways to travel while clapping (eg bounce, hop or gallop).

Elephant extravaganza:
Stand up! Trunks out!
Make large elephant shapes with wide flat feet and broad bent backs. Extend one arm slowly forward to form a long, dangling trunk.
Left, right, left, right.
Walk from flat foot to flat foot in time to a slow, strong steady beat.
Water, water everywhere.
Practise using trunks, standing in wide bent shapes. Stoop forward and curl one arm inwards towards the

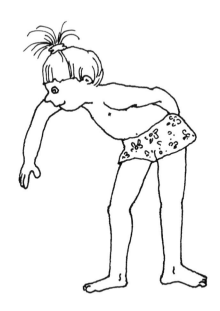

chin. Slowly stand up straight, extending the 'trunk' high in the air and pretend to spray water. Repeat these curling and uncurling actions several times.

Trunks and tails.

Have a 'trunks and tails' parade. The elephants each plod towards a partner, then stand one behind the other, holding one arm out in front for a trunk, the other arm behind for a tail. They join trunks and tails by holding hands and then plod, jog and dance together as one enormous line of elephants.

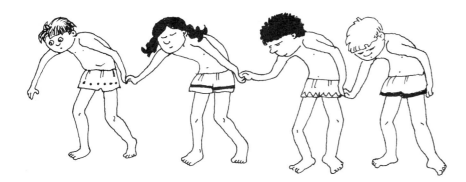

The aviary:
Baby bird fluffs its feathers and swoops . . .
Wriggle upwards into a wide stretched shape, then stop still for a second before running into a low shape.

. . . flies and flutters . . .
Run with arms rising and stretching, sinking and closing. Encourage stillness between the actions with only eyelids and fingers fluttering.

. . . plays hide and seek . . .
Stop still in spaces after running and fluttering at high and low levels.

. . . and finally settles.
Sink and settle slowly to the ground with arms curled around bodies.

Penguin parade:
The penguins waddle . . .
Make small squat shapes and waddle round the room with turned out, flat flapping feet and puffed out tummies.
. . . splash and jump.
Make short, bouncy, flat-footed jumps forwards, 'splashing' with flat, floppy hands.

The kangaroo makes big bouncy jumps . . .
The jumps must start and finish with bent knees and with fists and elbows bent high in front of chests.
. . . and little, light jumps.
Make fast, light jumps from two feet to two feet, forwards, backwards and sideways.

Mischievous monkeys are amazing acrobats.
Stand with arms dangling to knees and swinging loosely from side to side, jogging from one foot to the other. Make various balancing, jumping, falling and rolling actions.

The royal march of the lion.
March round the room with head held high, toes pointed and arms clawing the air.
Rising and roaring.
Rise upwards, lifting head to face the ceiling, and roar.
Long, light runs.
Take big, light running steps with long stretched legs. Ask for soft padding from foot to foot.

The crafty crocodile:
Gigantic claws and jaws.
Move with outstretched arms and fingers, snapping them open and shut.
Crocodile lines.
Form lines of three with the front person as the 'snappy jaws', the middle one as the 'spiky claws' and the back one as the 'big, bent back legs'.
The crafty crocodile makes a move!
Step slowly and strongly in crocodile lines with 'snappy jaws', 'spiky claws' and 'big bent back legs'. Change so that all members of the group have the chance to lead.

Graceful giraffes.
Take slow smooth steps on tiptoes with stretched necks, arms and legs and graceful movements.

Carnival of the animals.
Choose one child to be leader. As the leader passes by, each child joins the line. When one long class line has been made, the leader marches like a lion with everyone else marching behind. Change leaders frequently, introducing a new animal activity for each new leader.

The Three Little Pigs

Age range
Three to seven.

Emphasis
Working actions and group formations.

Pigs at play.
Trot on tiptoes with high knees and hands held in front of chests, in and out of spaces to form a follow-my-leader line. Skip and wave, one behind the other, then tiptoe away from the line into spaces.

Gathering the straw.
Make wide scooping gestures, then step to form a class group in the centre of the room. Finish by sinking together to the ground.
A round straw house.
Rise slowly upwards then spread out to form one large class circle.
The big bad wolf creeps stealthily.
Choose one child to be the wolf. Everyone stays completely still as the 'wolf' creeps silently round the circle, steps into the centre and stands looking fierce.
He huffed, and he puffed . . .
Everyone joins in with the exaggerated puffing and blowing actions in time to the words.
. . . and he blew the house down!
Make one last blowing action and whirl slowly or quickly up and down, away from the circle into spaces. Finish with slow spiralling movements down to the ground.

A house made of sticks:
Chopping wood.
Make repetitive, rhythmic actions from high to low and forwards and backwards. Reinforce the beat and emphasise the size and strength of the actions.
Bundles of sticks.
Carry or drag 'sticks' towards two other children to form groups of three.
A crooked stick house.
Start curled up together in groups of three, then grow upwards and outwards with sudden staccato actions using elbows, knees and fingers to form a spiky, irregular group shape.
He huffed and he puffed . . .
One child as the wolf creeps around the crooked house shapes. The groups suddenly change shape on the words 'huffed' and 'puffed'.
. . . and he blew the house down!
Make sudden spiky jumps away from the group into spaces followed by a sudden jump and fall to the ground.

A house made of bricks:
Staggering and carrying.
Stand in the centre of the room with the children staggering towards you, then away again to a space. Repeat this a few times until finally they all join together round you to form a class group.
The house gets bigger and bigger.
The group grows upwards a little bit, then a bit more, and finally stretches up tall.
A wide wide wall.
The group steps and stretches sideways to form a wall. Repeat this until the class can form a line which divides the room space.
'Little pig, little pig, let me in.'
Playing the part of the wolf, creep towards, away from, and around the class wall shape.
He huffed and he puffed.
The class wall moves into a line and creeps quietly round and round the wolf until a class circle shape is formed.
Aha! The wolf is trapped inside the house of bricks!

Crazy chickens

Age range
Three to eight.

Emphasis
Using the words 'strut', 'flap', 'settle', 'scratch' and 'peck' to discover different travelling actions.

The cockerel struts.
Step slowly in and out of spaces, with knees lifted strongly, arms moving sharply up and down and head moving jerkily forwards and backwards.

Flapping (perhaps one chicken has lost an egg and everyone has to search for it).
Run and jump quickly in and out of spaces with arms flapping quickly and sharply up and down. Repeat, with feet shaking during each jump.

Settling.
Turn slowly and gently, around and down into a small round shape, as though curled up or sitting on a nest.

Scratching.
Run quickly in and out of the spaces, pausing sometimes to scratch slowly at the floor with one foot. Watch that foot closely. Change direction after every scratch.

Form a class circle then make one large, slow scratch on the floor together, watching the foot closely before running quickly to the centre. Then run back to the outside of the circle to scratch again. Turn and start again.

Pecking.
As above, but instead of scratching make one large, fast peck towards the floor with the head. When pausing to peck, bend the knees and turn in the toes.

Old MacDonald's Farm

Age range
Three to six.

Emphasis
Contrasting actions, level and speed.

Old MacDonald had a farm E I E I O.
Stomp from space to space as if wearing big wellington boots.

And on that farm he had some . . .
Stamp round and round the room to form one large class circle then all shrink down towards the floor.

. . . chickens (scurrying round the farmyard).
Start from the floor with bent elbows and nodding heads, then wriggle upwards and scurry from space to space. Emphasise changes in direction by introducing statue stops.

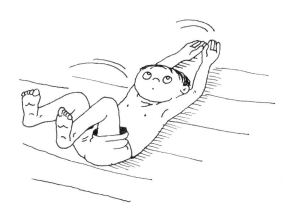

. . . rabbits (jumping through the fields).
Start with legs bent and hands held high in front of the chest, then take long leaps with arms and legs outstretched.

. . . pigs (rolling in sticky, squashy mud).
Curl and stretch, first on backs, then on fronts. Introduce slow, rhythmic rolling actions from side to side and over and over.

. . . birds (swooping, hovering, whirling and settling).
Grow slowly from small curled shapes to wide stretched
shapes, then swoop from high to low levels. Hover on the
spot with arms fluttering, and whirl round and round.
Finally, settle back slowly into small curled body shapes.
Improve the quality by asking for heads to be held high
and stressing the light sudden actions of birds.
. . . horses (trotting and galloping).
Trot on the spot with heads and knees held high, then trot
rhythmically from space to space.
. . . Old MacDonald had a farm, E I E I O.
Stamp round and round the room, finishing by forming
one final class circle.

The Emperor and the Nightingale

'The Emperor loved the song of the nightingale. He
removed the nightingale from the magic garden where it
lived and put it in a cage . . ..'

Age range
Seven to eleven.

Emphasis
Exploring the space close to, and far away from, the
centre of the body.

Trapped inside a round, golden cage!
Work individually or in pairs. Take long slow steps or
short, quick careful steps on a circular pathway,
sometimes pausing and turning slowly to look behind.
**The key to the cage hangs on a large hook. Can you
reach through the bars and take it?**
Step round the circle as before, sometimes pausing to
reach sideways, forwards, backwards or above the head
into a stretched, balanced shape.
No luck! Panic! Could you bounce the door open?
Run swiftly on a short straight pathway, then turn quickly
and powerfully to run back to the starting place.
    Repeat this, running as above, turning high then low;
turning on two feet then on one foot; turning on-balance
then off-balance.
Perhaps you could pull open the bars?
Work in pairs, standing next to each other in a tall
straight shape and holding hands, arms above heads,
then pulling slowly and powerfully, take one large step
sideways away from the partner, ending in a wide low
shape.

Stand facing each other in tall straight shapes holding hands, then pulling slowly and powerfully, take one large step backwards away from the partner, ending in a low crouched shape.

Stand back to back holding hands, then pull away from each other and take one large step forwards, ending in a long low shape.

Finally, stand next to, facing, or back to back with a partner in a tall straight shape. Join hands above the head then lean slowly and powerfully away from each other, hands joined, with the hips, back or tummy leading, but keeping feet still.

Hooray! We've pulled the bars of the cage apart!
Divide the class into two groups with one half 'opening the bars' in pairs and the other half running or jumping through the 'bars' as they travel around the space.

Form groups of three or four, then take it in turns to 'open the bars' in pairs so that the other children in the group can crouch down low, ready to run or jump 'through the bars' when they see the widest gap possible.

Escape at last!
Run, jump and twirl quickly from space to space, with arms flapping away from or fluttering near to the body, choosing the best route back to the magic garden. Repeat the above sequence, sometimes pausing to change direction, stooping low or stretching high.

Finish far away from each other or form groups which hover in a flock formation, some high and some low.

Flight

In this chapter the emphasis is on lightness, buoyancy, elevation and height. These are explored through a variety of images ranging from simple starting points such as kites, through parachutes, to more complex flying machines and the antics of 'superpeople'.

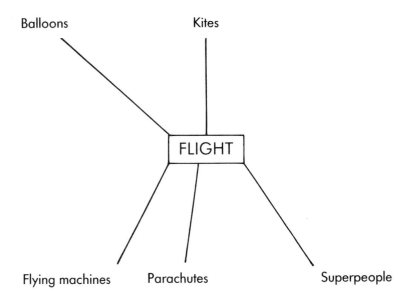

Balloons

Age range
Three to seven.

Emphasis
Contrasting shapes, sizes and levels.

Blowing up balloons.
Make three long blows, using the hands to show the shape of the inflating balloon.
Balloon shapes.
Start from a low, curled position then grow slowly into round, tall or twisted shapes.
Shrinking and growing.
Work at different speeds, contrasting slow growing with fast shrinking and vice versa.
Round balloon shapes.
Stand with rounded arms, puffed cheeks and tummies and wide legs.

Bouncing balloons.
Jump high from space to space. Ensure the shape is kept throughout.
Throwing and catching.
Jump suddenly and powerfully with arms raised high, then sink slowly and gently lowering arms. Repeat, throwing balloons to a partner.
Popping balloons.
Bounce lightly down on to the floor.
Letting the air out.
Choose a balloon shape then, at a given signal, shrink and turn down to the floor.

The story of an escaped balloon.
The balloon is blown up.
Choose and make a variety of balloon shapes.
It bounces along the ground.

Develop jumping on one spot, forwards, backwards and sideways.
The wind blows the balloon high in the air.
Incorporate rising, falling, and turning actions as the balloon is whirled along by the wind.
Stuck in a tree!
Select an inflated balloon shape. With feet firmly on the ground, choose one body part to represent the string being stuck in the tree. Pull sideways, backwards and forwards keeping the chosen body part taut.
Trying to get free.
Pull and tug this way and that to try to break free.
Pop!
Make one sudden jump then collapse on to the ground.
Or – 'The great escape'.
Rise up high, then turn and whirl freely from one space to the next.

Kites

Age range
Five to eleven.

Emphasis
Using words to focus on lightness and height.

Kites float, flutter, hover, rise, swoop, curve, glide and land.
Run swiftly along curved pathways, turning gently upwards and downwards. Encourage careful stepping and balancing with wide and waving arms and legs.

Join together in pairs or groups to form a kite tail or represent a box, frame or flat kite.

Flying machines

Roll up, roll up! Presenting a most daring, death-defying display in bravely buffetting bi-planes of amazingly accurate aerobatics by the (class name) fabulously fearless flying team!

Age range
Seven to eleven.

Emphasis
Humorous balancing activities.

Hold on tight – the runway is full of bumps and holes!
Crouch near the floor in pairs, one behind the other, shaking and shuddering, rocking forwards, backwards and sideways. Continue, sometimes sharply lifting the

hips and ducking the head, sometimes jumping together quickly in a small round shape.

Take-off.
Crouch near the floor, then slowly and carefully sit down and roll slowly backwards until both legs and arms are held in the air over the head.

Switch on the automatic pilot!
Getting out of the cockpit.
From the take-off shape, roll slowly forwards till sitting, then slowly and carefully stand up.

Wing-walking
- Step slowly and carefully on tiptoes, using arms to balance, along a short straight pathway looking upwards. Repeat, taking long or short steps backwards and forwards with arms held high.

- Crouch carefully into a small, low shape, then grow into a balance on one foot.
- Turn carefully on one or both feet.
- Make a careful roll.
- Quickly, lightly and carefully jump on the spot, pointing toes in the air, and landing softly with bent knees.

Don't fall off!
Wobble vigorously on tiptoes with knees bent, forwards, backwards or sideways.

Wing-walking with the team.
Form pairs or small groups and make a sequence based on the wing-walking ideas practised previously. The team could follow a leader or perform different tricks, perhaps going under, over or around each other.

The grand finale – Wave to the crowd!
Make an amazing group shape: side by side, one behind the other, or a pyramid, for example.

Parachutes

Age range
Seven to eleven.

Emphasis
Contrasting group shapes on the floor and standing.

Out of the plane.
Jump powerfully, knees high, landing in small, crouched shapes, then roll slowly backwards, finishing on knees or tummy.

Free-falling.
Rock slowly and smoothly on tummy or back, arms and legs held away from the floor and waving gently. Roll slowly backwards or sideways, keeping arms and legs away from the floor before rolling slowly backwards or sideways towards a partner or small group.

Formation falling.
Still in pairs or groups, rock slowly and smoothly on tummy or back with arms and legs held away from the floor.

Please don't let go!
Roll slowly and smoothly backwards or sideways, joined by the wrists or ankles to a partner or in a small group.
Opening the parachute.
Stand on both feet, knees slightly bent and arms raised above the head. Sway gently forwards, backwards, sideways and around, slowly and smoothly bending, stretching, twisting and turning.

Don't come so close!
Make a tangled group shape with arms and legs intertwined and bodies twisted under, over and around each other at high, medium and low levels.
A small gust of wind.
Take several small, quick light steps, or one large soft jump to a new space.

A thermal.
Stretch quickly and strongly into large balanced shapes, before turning down into small twisted shapes.

A perfect landing.
Jump gently on the spot, slowly and smoothly crouching and rolling to finish on knees or feet.

. . . or stuck in the trees!
Move as though hooked to the branch of a tree, keeping one body part still – hand, elbow, hips, knees or foot – while wriggling and shaking the rest of the body.

Superpeople

Age range
Five to eleven.

Emphasis
Exaggerated body shapes, speed and strength.

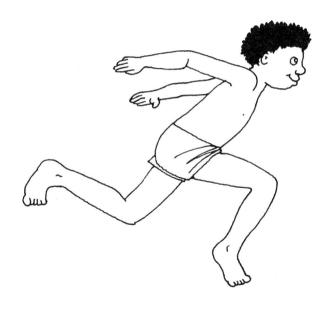

Whoosh . . . to the rescue!
Take fast, light running steps along a winding pathway, with arms outstretched behind like a cloak.

Zooooom!
With knees bent and back curved forward, hands clenched in two fists and arms stretched forward, take quick, light running steps, sometimes stopping in clear 'zooming' shapes before changing direction. Try balancing on one foot on each stopping shape.

Take-off to trouble.
Make take-off shapes: hands in two fists, one arm outstretched above the head, the other arm bent close to the body, one leg bending with flexed foot, the other leg stretched. Then run quickly and lightly, stopping to balance in take-off shapes.

Deflecting bullets with indestructible wrist and ankle bands.
Stand on both feet, knees and elbows slightly bent. Lift feet high or stretch wrists low, twisting, turning and balancing very quickly.

Speeding to the scene of toppling tower-blocks, rumbling avalanches, runaway trains.
Make slow, strong, pushing movements with hands and

arms, stretching forwards, sideways, backwards, upwards and down. Make slow, strong pushing movements with other body parts: feet, hips, back etc.

Burning buildings, flaming forests, smouldering streets.
Start in a crouched shape near the floor and breath in, growing into a wide, stretched shape. Then blow out the air, shrinking slowly and strongly down to the floor.

'Newsflash! Here is the latest video, straight from the disaster area – slowed down so that you can see Superperson clearly.'
Take huge, exaggerated, running steps, slowly and smoothly lifting one knee, bringing the leg through and stretching it as far forwards as possible before placing the foot on the floor to continue the slow running sequence.

Bionic pairs and dazzling duos.
Form pairs and try some of Superperson's sensational stunts together.

Magic, mystery and monsters

The swirl of a magic cloak, a flying broomstick or a magical spell can 'transform' young children into whatever they wish to be. Older children are spellbound by tales such as 'Aladdin and his Magic Lamp' and by images of haunted houses or mysterious monsters.

The starting points require the children to put themselves into fantasy situations.

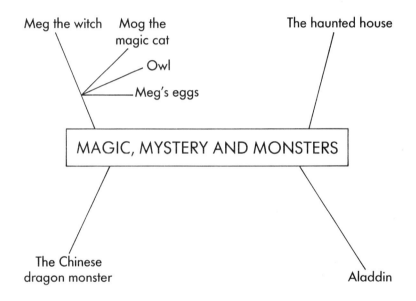

Meg the witch   Mog the magic cat   The haunted house

Owl

Meg's eggs

MAGIC, MYSTERY AND MONSTERS

The Chinese dragon monster   Aladdin

Meg the witch

Age range
Three to seven.

Emphasis
Crooked and spiky body shapes.

Witch shapes.
Crouch down, then grow slowly upwards into a crooked shape.
Crooked walks.
Walk knock-kneed then with high pointed knees and long stretched fingers.
Flying on broomsticks:
'Rise up high, swoosh down low,
Whooshing, swooshing, witches go!'
Stretch out arms as if holding a broomstick. Take little, light, running steps, rising up high, then sinking down low, with arms wide and outstretched, then low and closed. Accompany the action with the 'whooshing, swooshing' words.

Mog the magic cat

Age range
Three to seven.

Emphasis
Long and stretched body shapes.

Making cat shapes.
Curl, arch or stretch from low shapes on the floor to wide outstretched shapes on hands and feet, or high on tiptoes.

Paws and claws.
Curl hands in front of chests like paws, then suddenly, percussively, pop each finger out of a fist in turn, first one hand then with the other. Try extending and curling toes too!

Cats creeping.
Creep from one foot to the other with paws clawing the air, or from foot to foot and hand to hand.

Owl

Age range
Three to seven.

Emphasis
Large, round body shapes.

A big, fluffy round shape.
Form small shapes in crouched positions with knees tucked up to chins and elbows close into sides. Develop this slowly into round shapes with puffed cheeks, bloated tummies and elbow wings sticking outwards.

Creeping and leaping.
Form phrases of creeping and leaping. Emphasise the long stretched leaps which break up the creeping.
A crazy cat.
Use the illustrations from the Meg and Mog books to encourage children to form crooked, irregular spiky shapes and develop ways of moving backwards and sideways in those shapes.

Owl jumps.
Make little light jumps with feet together. Form phrases where Owl jumps, stops and flutters its elbow wings and fingers.

Meg, Mog and Owl.
Contrast the actions of spiky crooked Meg, long lean Mog and fat fluffy Owl. Work in threes as the characters in different body shapes.

Meg's eggs

Age range
Three to seven.

Emphasis
Different ways of travelling.

Out with the cauldron! It's time to make a supper spell. In go the scuttling lizards.
The children move around on all fours, quickly and lightly, forwards, sideways, backwards and round and round.

Next slide in the slithering newts.
Slither on tummies or backs, slowly and powerfully, forwards and backwards. Roll slowly over and over.

Add some bouncing frogs – boing! Quick, put the lid on!
Crouch low on two feet, then jump powerfully from space to space, high into the air with stretched knees, landing carefully with wide bent knees.
The magic mixture's brewing.
Choose whether to scuttle like lizards, slither like newts or jump like frogs. Pause sometimes to change from one creature to another.

Stir with a big, magic spoon.
Crouch low, slowly and powerfully circling arms in front, hands clenched together.
Bang! Meg's blown her magic spell!
Make one big, stretched jump, quickly and powerfully, into the air.
Three enormous eggs appear. Meg, Mog and Owl are starving: tap the eggs to try to break them.
Make quick, sharp tapping gestures forwards, backwards, to the sides, high and low, using different body parts: fingers, elbows, knees and toes.

That didn't work. Try rolling the eggs.
Roll quickly from place to place, sometimes curled up and sometimes making a long thin shape.

No good! Break the eggs by bouncing them.
Jump, sometimes taking off from one foot or both feet, sometimes landing on one foot or both feet, forwards, backwards, sideways and round and round.
The eggs still won't break. Let's see the best, most brilliant ideas – break those eggs wide open!
Make sharp tapping, quick rolling and powerful jumping actions, changing from one to another.

Help! Huge monsters are hatching out of the eggs!
From a small curled shape, push outwards slowly and powerfully with different body parts, such as hands, feet, back or hips, finishing in a large stretched shape.
Dangerous dinosaurs make the ground tremble.
Take huge, slow powerful steps – forwards, backwards, sideways and round and round, using hands as huge claws that slash the air.
Big claws and sharp teeth.
Clench both fists tightly then shoot out fingers one by one and stretch upwards with spiky claws leading. Use

arms and claw-like fingers to form a huge mouth which opens and closes.

Sharp spiky horns.

Shoot out elbows, knees and fingers to form a spiky upright shape, then take spiky steps with claws held high.

Long tails.

Work in pairs one behind the other with the front person using their arms as jaws, the back person using their arms to imitate a long swishing tail.

Moving monsters.

Step together in pairs with 'jaws' gnashing and 'tails' swishing. Change over so that everyone has the chance to be both jaws and tails.

Dangerous dinosaurs grow and grow.

Work in groups or as a class. Stand one behind the other, holding on to the shoulders of the person in front, and take huge, powerful, rhythmic steps together.

Meg makes a special shrinking spell.

From a large stretched shape, shrink slowly into a small curled shape on the floor.

Phew! That was close!

The haunted house

Age range
Five to eleven.

Emphasis
Contrasts in pathway, level and shape.

In a dark, dark forest.
Take big, slow silent steps with pauses in and out of spaces.

Forest pathways.
Draw long straight lines on the floor with chalk then tiptoe along, between, around and in and out of these straight lines to form curved pathways.

Night creatures.
Divide the class into two: one group turns into stretched, spiky night-time trees and the other jumping owls or running rats; one group stays still, the other jumps or scurries in and out of spaces.

The dark haunted house:
A creaking door.
Creep to a space then step forward and slowly but strongly push the door with hands, arms and legs.

Searching high and low.
Take quiet, tiptoe steps with statue stops at high and low levels.

Cobweb shapes.
Grow slowly from curled to wide shapes, stretching and reaching at different levels.

Scuttling spiders.
Stretch on to hands and feet and scuttle sideways.

The spiral staircase.
Start by using one finger to draw a spiral shape in the air from high to low levels. Slowly rise and sink with curling and turning actions from high to low levels. Lastly, tiptoe round and round in small circles.

Ghostly creatures:
A whispy, whirling ghost.
Start in curled shapes on the floor then grow slowly upwards into tall stretched shapes, curling and turning slowly and lightly in and out of the spaces.
Skeletons: bony arms.
Stand with loose, limp shoulders, bent elbows and floppy fingers.

Rattling kneebones.
Shake knees from side to side and up and down.
Shaking skulls.
Nod heads up and down and from side to side.
Dancing skeletons.
Use different body parts to lead varied travelling activities from space to space, eg hopping with high bony knees, jumping with jerky elbows and stepping with stretched feet.
A big, black cat.
Curl and stretch 'paws', then whole bodies; run and stop with 'paws' held high in the air, with sudden statue stops and frequent changes in direction; creep and pounce.
Form a phrase of movement, eg creep, creep, creep and pounce.

Which way out?
Through long straight corridors?
Run along straight pathways with sudden statue stops and clear changes in direction.
Down the spiral staircase?
Creep round and round in small circles, turning slowly from high wide to low curled shapes.
Through the spider's web?
Half the class stretches and reaches to make a cobweb shape and the other half steps carefully high and low in and out of the web.
Out of the door?
Make slow, strong pushing actions, followed by fast, light running steps.

The Chinese dragon monster

Long ago, in China, a huge dragon monster lived in the slime at the bottom of a muddy river. From time to time, the monster rose from the river and advanced on the villages nearby, killing and eating the people who lived there. Eventually they realised that the dragon monster appeared at regular intervals – once a year. They also discovered that the dragon monster was frightened by loud noises, fire and bright colours (red, pink and especially orange). So one year, the villagers prepared themselves for the dragon monster's appearance. Making loud noises, waving flame sticks and flags of brightly coloured cloth, they drove the dragon monster back into the river. It was never seen again. The dragon monster's defeat is celebrated at Chinese New Year, with brightly coloured flags, firecrackers, parties and carnivals.

Age range
Five to eleven.

Emphasis
Contrasts in strength and speed; exaggerated body shapes.

The dragon monster rises from the river and advances on the villages, killing and eating the people.
Run swiftly with large powerful movements in and out of the spaces, then freeze in the biggest shape possible. Suggest the following ways of making shapes bigger:
● Stretch out fingers and toes as far as possible.
● Stand on one foot and stretch the other one out.
● Lie on the floor.
The dragon monster is as tall as a tree, as wide as the school, and as long as a train. It lives in the slime at

- Step, jump and slither across the floor.
Take care when stepping or jumping and make sure that there isn't anyone slithering underneath.

The dragon monster frightens the villagers. How?
Decide how to finish the sequence.
- In a big terrifying shape?
- Hovering over a frightened villager?
- Flattening a house with one huge jump?

The villagers flee from the dragon monster and hide!
Run swiftly in and out of spaces and then make a shape

the bottom of the river.
Rise slowly and powerfully from the floor into big shapes.

The slime is heavy and the water is deep.
Repeat the pushing movements, even more slowly and powerfully.

The dragon monster is hungry. How will it travel to the nearby villages?
Change from one sort of travelling to another.
- Large, slow powerful steps;
- Large powerful jumps;
- Slow, powerful slithering on the tummy;

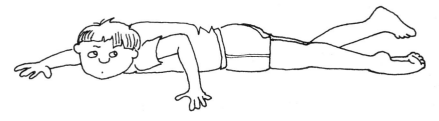

81

Change spontaneously from fast shaking to a small hidden shape.

Form pairs, one as the dragon monster, the other a frightened villager. Begin some way away from each other, and finish near each other in a big/small shape.

Frightening the dragon monster:

Stamping and clapping.

Play a rhythmic drumbeat and emphasise the need to listen first, and then clap and stamp.

Advancing and retreating.

Step forwards and backwards, towards and away from a partner. Form a sequence of stepping actions where four steps are taken each time.

as though hiding behind a small bush. Repeat this as though hiding behind a tall thin tree. Repeat, this time choosing a shape to hide behind.

Talk about the villagers. What do people do when they are frightened? They shake.

Shake different body parts as fast as possible; head, shoulders, hands, feet, knees, hips.

They hide.

Curl up into a small shape as quickly as possible.

Aladdin

Age range
Seven to eleven.

Emphasis
Straight and curved body shapes, floor and air patterns.

Aladdin lazily draws patterns in the sand.
Sit and use fingers then toes to draw straight and curvy lines. Draw patterns on the floor all around the body. Try making patterns in the air.

An enormous dragon monster moves slowly towards the village.
Form shapes in pairs and then in a class line, moving together in as many different ways as possible.
The villagers frighten the dragon monster away.
Use very quick clapping, stamping, jumping and waving actions.
A celebration dance – 'Happy New Year!'
Skip and turn in and out of spaces and finish by dancing in a class circle shape.

The wicked magician.
Rise slowly into a tall strong shape with shifty eyes which move from side to side.

The magician strides and shuffles along.
Contrast strong, bold strides using arms to imitate a cloak flowing behind; or short, shifty shuffling steps with arms as a cloak pulled around the body.

The magic cave: a big, black hole appears in the ground.
Start from a crouched position and use one long, stretched finger to draw a big circle slowly on the ground. Step carefully around the outer edge of the circle. Stretch arms wide like a magician's cloak opening and jump low down to the ground as if falling into a deep dark hole.

Try to find a way out.
Tremble and shake as though with fear, feeling all around and pushing upwards, sideways, downwards, backwards with strong, flat hands.

The genie of the ring.
Rub hands together slowly round and round then move slowly, curling arms and hands and rising upwards, turning and whirling the whole body high and low in and out of the spaces.

The genie of the lamp.
Jump, feet together, in and out of spaces. Encourage explosive, firecracker jumps with darting, stabbing fingers.

The wicked magician arrives in disguise. New lamps for old!
Revise the original movement image of the magician by practising the following sequence of movements:
- Growing tall and stretching wide;
- Taking long stretched strides in a wide body shape;
- Shrinking to form a closed body shape;
- Shuffling in closed body shapes.

Aladdin and the wicked magician.
Form pairs, one person as Aladdin, the other as the wicked magician. 'Aladdin' curls up small; the 'magician' grows tall and stretched. The 'magician' waves the 'magic lamp' high in the air whilst creeping and laughing round 'Aladdin'. 'Aladdin' takes a sudden, high explosive leap towards the raised hand, snatches the 'lamp' and the 'magician' collapses to the ground.
Happy again.
Skip in pairs as Aladdin and the princess or skip around each other individually.

Fire and light

The themes of fire and light are ideal for a variety of different dance ideas. The image of fire provides contrasts between sparks and flames which move in a quick, direct way, and smoke which complements this by rising and sinking, curling and whirling, slowly and lightly.

Light is represented through candles, a candlelit procession, mirrors and shadows.

This theme has strong links with religious festivals such as Christmas, Diwali and Hanukkah. There are also links with pagan festivals, such as the shadows created at Stonehenge on Midsummer's Day, with birthday celebrations and firework parties.

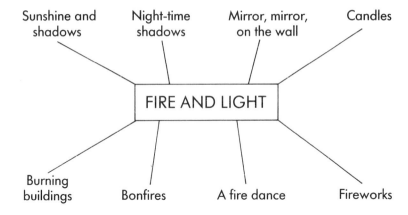

Sunshine and shadows

Shadow, shadow, curled up small,
I can make you grow up tall.
Now I'm jumping stretched and wide,
Shadow, shadow, at my side.
Tiptoe slowly, shadow go!
I can't lose my shadow, though.

Kate Harrison

Age range
Five to eleven.

Emphasis
Follow-my-leader activities.

Encourage the children to say the words of the poem as they move. Introduce relationships by first having the class facing you.

Shadow, shadow, curled up small,
Start in a variety of low, curled shapes.
I can make you grow up tall.
Grow slowly into tall shapes, or into thin shapes along the ground. Try this in pairs; stress moving at the same time and into the same shapes.
Now I'm jumping stretched and wide.
Jump with legs wide apart and arms outstretched, either mirroring a partner, standing side by side or in follow-my-leader formation.

Shadow, shadow, at my side,
Develop a jumping shadow sequence with the emphasis on moving simultaneously into exactly the same shapes.
Tiptoe slowly, shadow go!
Take big, slow controlled steps to a space, dodging and darting in different directions with sudden statue stops, before finally returning to partners.
I can't lose my shadow, though!
Make follow-my-leader shadows. Introduce meeting and parting in big/small shapes at low/high levels; growing and shrinking into tall, wide, twisted and spiky shadowy shapes; moving lightly one after the other, first slowly then quickly. Explore moving together at the same time or one after the other. Try to catch each other out by moving unpredictably!

Night-time shadows

Age range
Three to seven.

Emphasis
Contrasting quick and jerky, soft and smooth movements.

Spiky spooky shadows.
Make sudden jerky actions with fingers, elbows, knees and head.
Silent slinking shadows.
Work in pairs. The person in front leads with slow, controlled steps from space to space.
The shadows play with the moon.
Choose any shape – spiky, tall, wide, round – but emphasise the quality. Emphasise moving one at a time and freezing in a clear body shape, jumping, skipping and turning with a partner meeting and parting and making sideways formations.

Mirror, mirror, on the wall

Age range
Seven to eleven.

Emphasis
Stretched, twisted, spiky and amusing body shapes in turn.

The magic mirror.
In pairs, face each other and grow then shrink together, slowly and smoothly, into alternate tall, wide, twisted and low curled, body shapes. Develop this by using simple symmetric and asymmetric shapes, mirroring each other's actions exactly.

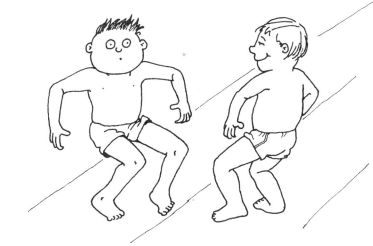

The hall of mirrors.
Again facing each other, jump high and low and from side to side into a variety of amusing body shapes. Change level and use words such as wobbly, spiky, thin, fat and crooked to gain quality. This activity could develop into a 'hall of mirrors' dance: two people dance facing each other and stop in a variety of odd mirroring shapes each time the music stops.
The mirror cracks from side to side.
Encourage sudden jerking of body parts to form spiky shapes, then jumping from side to side and from high to low.

Candles

Age range
Five to eleven.

Emphasis
Growing and shrinking shapes; processing in pairs, lines and group formations.

Candles come in all shapes and sizes:
Tall thin candles.
Grow from a small shape near the floor, slowly and smoothly into a tall thin shape on tiptoes, arms stretched and fingers pointed; or lie on the floor and raise legs up, slowly and smoothly into a tall thin shape, supporting the body on shoulders with toes stretched towards the ceiling.

Pyramid candles.
From a small shape near the floor, grow slowly and smoothly into a tall triangular shape, feet wide apart, arms raised and fingers reaching above the head; or start with both hands and one foot on the floor, then grow slowly and smoothly into a triangular shape, one foot stretching towards the ceiling. Repeat this with both feet and one hand wide apart on the floor, one hand stretched towards the ceiling.
Tall twisted candles.
Turn slowly and smoothly, hands leading, around and upwards into a tall twisted shape.
Short spiralled candles.
Turn slowly and smoothly, wrapping arms around bodies into a short twisted shape. Then turn back the other way into another short twisted shape.
The flame wavers as people move about the room.
Choose one of the candle shapes, then make the 'flame'

shapes, reaching arms and legs towards the ceiling, stretching fingers and toes. Encourage each group member to grow into a different shape.

Candles on a birthday cake.

Make a class or small group circle, growing into candle shapes.

A candle-lit procession.

Walk slowly and carefully, hands reaching out forwards with palms up, as if holding a precious candle. Repeat this, leading or following a partner, a class line or a small group formation, walking slowly and carefully on different pathways – curved, winding paths, circles or spirals.

(hands, feet or even head) move gently from side to side. Gently and smoothly wave the 'flame' so far that the rest of the body begins to sway.

A door opens and the flame flickers in the draught.

Retain the candle shapes, shaking the 'flame' quickly and jerkily.

Some candles are snuffed out.

From candle shapes, quickly shrink into small shapes near the floor.

Some candles melt until the flame dies.

Sink slowly down, then spread out into a large flat shape on the floor.

On special occasions, a special candleholder is used with several candles . . .

From a small shape on the floor, slowly and strongly stretch arms and legs, one at a time or all together, towards the ceiling, stretching fingers and toes.

. . . or many candles.

Form small groups, then grow slowly into candle

Fireworks

Age range
Three to nine.

Emphasis
Contrasting dynamics and body shapes.

Sizzling sparklers that burn . . .
Choose whether to sit or stand and shake hands quickly and strongly in front, behind, at the sides, high, low and all around.

. . . and flash.
Stand, making hands into a fist shape, then strongly and sharply stretch and flick the fingers out in front, behind, at the sides, high and low, both hands together or at different times in different places.

Rushing rockets that fly, . . .
Run quickly on different pathways.
. . . explode . . .
Jump powerfully into clear star shapes.
. . . and fizzle.
Turn gently to settle on the floor.
Whirling wheels that whizz round . . .
Pedal legs in the air, quickly and strongly.

. . . and round . . .
Circle straight arms, quickly and strongly, sometimes forwards and sometimes backwards.
. . . and round.
Turn quickly from place to place, one way and then the other.
Some fireworks don't light properly.
Repeat the above, sometimes drooping quickly or collapsing slowly on to the floor.

Be careful! Back away!
Step backwards slowly and carefully. Choose one person to be 'the firework that won't light properly' and form a circle around that person. As the 'firework' stops and starts, everyone else steps slowly away backwards, holding hands for as long as possible.

Will the firework fizzle out?
The 'firework' slowly turns and settles.

Or explode?
Make one, big, powerful jump into a clear star shape.

Wait and watch until an adult says that the firework is safe.

At the community firework display, there are some large starbursts.
Form small groups which grow slowly into a group star shape in a circle, a line or a close group with pointed toes and fingers stretching out at every level and in every direction. Jump powerfully away from the group, then gently turn to settle on the floor, a long way from the group.

93

A fire dance

Age range
Five to nine.

Emphasis
Contrast between smooth and jerky actions.

The fire begins with one spark, then more and more dart everywhere.
Make short, sharp stabbing actions with fingers, elbows and knees, first on the spot, then jumping and darting high and low in and out of spaces.
Smoke rises; it whirls and curls around and around.
Form a curled body shape then rise, turn, open and spread out. Whirl from high to low around the space.
Flames shoot out in all directions.
Make sudden jumps into angular body shapes.

The flames are dancing – up and down and in and out of each other.
Jump from space to space using fingers, elbows and feet to lead the movement. Dance near to and away from each other.
The fire spreads very quickly . . .
Make either large, slow, curling, 'smoke' movements or short, sharp, 'flame' movements, first on the spot then spreading faster and faster through the space.
. . . then dies away. The smoke curls and puffs slowly, the flames are gone, the embers smoulder.
Slow the action down so that the 'flames' only move occasionally. The 'smoke' slowly curls its way back to a curled up body shape.

Bonfires

Age range
Five to nine.

Emphasis
Changing shapes; moving as a group.

We're building a bonfire. What shall we use? Things that no-one needs, things that are safe, such as big, fat, empty boxes.
Grow slowly into a large flat, or large twisted shape, arms stretched, knees slightly bent.
Broken twigs and branches.
Grow slowly into spiky balancing shapes, using as many joints as possible.
Old, chopped tree stumps.
Make large round shapes – either sitting or standing.
Scrunched-up newspaper.
Form small round shapes on the floor. Change quickly and sharply from one sort of shape to another.

Building the bonfire.
Work in pairs with one person pulling, pushing, turning, rolling or dragging a partner (who is in a shape as above), slowly and powerfully, to where the imaginary bonfire is to be. Then use different shapes as above, joining with others to make a group bonfire shape.
The bonfire is lit.
Sit in a class or group circle.
Warming hands. . .
Reach slowly forward with arms, stretching fingers towards the imaginary fire.
. . . and feet.
Balance on bottoms, stretching legs slowly forward and pointing toes.
   Stand in a class or group circle then reach slowly forward towards the centre into a balancing shape on one foot and/or reach slowly backwards, with one foot towards the centre of the circle, into a balancing shape.

Burning buildings

The Great New Tower is on fire! It is 100 floors high! The fire-ladders are not long enough! There is a power failure!

Age range
Seven to eleven.

Emphasis
Running, rolling, lifting and supporting with a partner.

No lights in the room. Where is the door?
Run quickly, sometimes turning suddenly to run another way.
No lights in the corridors. Is there a way to the lower floors?
Run quickly and carefully on straight pathways, making sharp changes of direction, leading or following a partner.
Get underneath the smoke.
Roll or slither slowly across the floor, individually or joined to a partner.

Ouch! That's hot!
Stretch hands and/or feet slowly towards the centre of the circle then quickly pull them away. Rub hands together vigorously in front, behind, at the sides and all around. Repeat this while turning quickly one way and then the other. Vigorously rub a foot while hopping quickly from one foot to the other. Stretch slowly, pull away quickly, rub, turn and hop at different times to each other in the circle.

The lift is stuck between floors. Can we get up to the next floor?
Jump powerfully, reaching high. Then carefully lift or support a partner to reach up high. Make a group shape supporting someone who is stretching upwards.

Look! There are people in the building next door. Perhaps we could climb on to the window ledge.
Stand on toes, feet together, knees bent, arms wide to balance. Slowly and gently step sideways to the edge of the ledge, slowly and gently returning to the starting shape. Pause and shake knees quickly.

It's a long way down. Feeling dizzy?
Pause and shake the whole body, leaning forwards, backwards and sideways.

Jump to the next building!
Stand on both feet, bend the knees, swing the arms, and jump along the floor, landing softly on two feet.

Form pairs or groups of three then attempt to help the others to jump further by pushing gently and to land softly by catching them gently around the shoulders or waist.

Get the rescued people inside to safety.
In pairs or in threes, carefully lift and carry, pull or drag a partner by the wrists or ankles along the floor to a safe place.

Mini-beasts

Movement and dance sessions offer lots of opportunities for children to imitate, exaggerate and understand the shape, size and characteristics of a multitude of mini-beasts.

Start by introducing mini-beasts using running, creeping, jumping, slithering and flying activities. Having familiarised the children with some of the different ways in which mini-beasts move, name specific creatures and explore their shape, size, behaviour and habitats in more detail.

One of the best ways for children to understand the changes which take place in a mini-beast's life cycle is through dancing activities. Investigate how mini-beasts move. Can they move backwards? Sideways? In a straight line? Along twisting pathways? Do their bodies change shape?

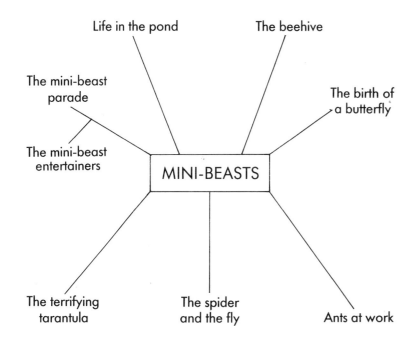

The mini-beast parade

Age range
Three to nine.

Emphasis
Contrasting travelling activities.

Running.
Take quick light steps from space to space with sudden statue stops and changes in direction.
Creeping.
Take slow, light, stretched steps on hands and feet.
Jumping.
Jump from both feet to both feet or from hands and feet to hands and feet.
Slithering.
Twist and curl slowly along the floor.

Flying.
Run high and low with high elbow wings (ie with the elbow as the highest point in this stretched shape) and with fast, fluttering arms. Introduce pauses and moments of stillness.

Crowds of creepy-crawlies.
Divide the class into four groups: creeping creatures, jumping creatures, flying creatures and slithering creatures. Choose a leader for each group and ask each group to stand in a corner of the room. Give the groups time to practise their actions moving from the corner towards the centre of the room. Accompany each group in turn so that they move one after the other towards the centre of the room. Form one long class line. Choose different leaders with the rest copying their actions one behind the other, ie a creeping, jumping, flying, running and slithering line.

Life in the pond

Age range
Five to eleven.

Emphasis
Curled, stretched and twisted body shapes; changes in
level and group formation.

The water of the pond is still. There is no sign of life . . .
Make a low, curled shape.
**. . . except for a ripple, a raindrop, a fish darting, a frog
jumping.**
Move lightly up and down into a new space with
sudden, spiky movements, jumping with knees and
elbows bent.
**There are floating water lilies. The flowers turn their
heads to the sun.**
Make floating movements which open and stretch
upwards and sideways towards a focal point.

The water spider spins a web among the water plants.
Divide the class into groups and work on circular floor
patterns. Form circles and criss-cross within the circles
to form a web.
**The water beetle swims under water on its front and on
its back; it flies about the pond.**
Move across the floor with smooth, creeping movements
first on fronts, then on backs, with arms and legs
splayed. Contrast this with gliding movements.
The spring pond is alive!
The groups choose one particular action, such as
'spiders' or 'beetles', then each one moves in turn.

The beehive

Age range
Five to nine.

Emphasis
Curled and stretched body shapes; changes in direction.

Buzz, the busy bee.
Make round body shapes with bent arms, then run, stop and 'buzz' by moving arms quickly up and down.

Building the honeycomb.
Move slowly forwards, backwards or sideways at high and low levels. Encourage stretching towards each other to create the feeling of linked shapes.

Inside the beehive.
Divide the class into two groups: one group as the honeycomb in stretched still shapes; the other as bees running and stopping in and out of the shapes.

Older children can use ropes which are pulled tightly to create a more realistic honeycomb. Change the groups around with the 'bees' moving from space to space along zig-zag pathways.

The birth of a butterfly

Age range
Five to eleven.

Emphasis
Changing body shapes; contrasts in activities and group formations.

Caterpillars.
Start from a variety of curled shapes on the ground and develop them into slow stretching, arching, shrinking and curling actions.

Weaving cocoons.
Turn slowly and spiral from low to high to low levels.

Wings unfolding.
Make strong pushing actions from curled shapes with elbows and arms slowly unfolding.

Wings fluttering.
Work on the spot with sudden fluttering actions of the arms and intermittent stops.

Butterflies.
Run and stretch upwards, then glide to a low level with arms closing around the body. Use the words 'fly', 'float' and 'settle' to improve the quality of action.

The life cycle of a butterfly.
Form groups of three or four. Allowing each group freedom of interpretation, work towards forming a complete repeatable sequence of movements using the activities practised before.

Ants at work

Age range
Three to seven.

Emphasis
Working in a group.

Searching for food.
Run quickly and quietly, stopping then changing direction.

Carrying loads.
Start in the centre of the room and take slow steps with bent backs away from and towards a central point. Finally, spread outwards around the edge of the room.

Making an enormous ant hill.
Choose one person to stand in the centre of the room with the rest in bent shapes around the edge. Then step slowly towards the one in the centre, making sure that no-one is too close to anyone else. Shrink slowly into small shapes on the floor.

Form an 'ant hill' by growing slowly upwards in time together with backs leading and heads tucked in. Repeat with those in the centre rising higher than the rest.

Flit, the fearless fly . . .
Rise on tiptoes with bent elbow wings and spiky fingers.
. . . flits from place to place.
Run quickly and quietly, stopping suddenly first high
then low.

The spider and the fly

Age range
Three to seven.

Emphasis
Creeping and running.

Long-legged super spider . . .
Stretching out on to hands and feet, or with feet spaced
wide apart, bend backs and reach out arms.
. . . steps slowly . . .
Make exaggerated steps with wide stretched feet and
fingers.
. . . and stretches and curls.
Stop in wide shapes, suddenly curling small.

Weaving a spider's web:
Stepping.
Form groups of three, then take slow, careful spider steps into curled up shapes facing each other.
Stretching.
Grow and spread slowly into wide stretched shapes.
Balancing.
Explore a variety of balancing actions so that one, two or three limbs can be released from the floor and are reaching and almost touching other stretched limbs to form the final shape.

Elasticated, group web shapes.
Use elastic to experiment with stretched web shapes. Reach high and low to form criss-cross patterns with the elastic.

Grow and shrink slowly into shapes together, and then stretch one at a time so that the web shape is formed strand by strand.

The terrifying tarantula

Age range
Five to eleven.

Emphasis
Group work; contrasts in shape and speed.

Bananas grow in big bunches.
- Stand in a space making 'banana' shapes, bending forwards, backwards or sideways, arms extended, hands and feet together, hips pushing outwards.

Caught in the spider's web.
Choose several groups to be wide web shapes (either with or without the elastic), and the rest 'flies'. The 'flies' run from space to space and the webs slowly change level and shape.

Encourage the 'flies' to run in and out of the spider's web and to stop and start on command.

A class cobweb.
Start spaced out in low, curled shapes. If you are using elastic then hold on to two pieces with each hand.

The cobweb grows and grows one strand at a time.
Choose one person to tiptoe among the others, touching heads gently one by one. When touched, stretch slowly into a variety of high, low and balanced shapes.

- Make stretched, curved 'banana' shapes, balancing on tummies, backs or sides, hands and feet together lifted off the floor.
- In pairs or small groups, find interesting ways of joining 'bananas' together, such as joining hands to hands, feet to feet or feet to hands. Try standing or balancing on the floor.
- Starting in a space, skip in and out of the spaces, joining the group 'banana bunch' one at a time.

A big bulging body and huge hairy legs.
Take long, low, creeping steps, arms slowly and smoothly curving through the air to suggest even more legs. Then creep round in a circle, backwards and sideways, with curving arms.

Still spiders sometimes pulsate.
Pause in a big, fat spider shape, with feet wide apart, knees bent, back curved over forwards, arms curved and wide apart. Arch and curve the back, and strongly and slowly ripple the arms and bend the knees.

Tiny tarantulas tread and turn.
One person as the 'terrifying tarantula' slowly creeps, pauses and pulsates while several 'tiny tarantulas' travel quickly and lightly around and under.

A terrifying tarantula seeking some shade.
Several people build 'banana bunch' shapes while the 'terrifying tarantula' moves under, over and through the group shape.

Freeze! Think! What's this? Can it be a big banana staring at me?
Hold the balancing shapes still.
Don't be silly! This is serious! That's a spider! Scram!
Starting from a still, stretched, balancing shape on one foot, suddenly run off quickly to another space. Finish either curled up or standing, shaking all over.

People passing stop for a snack.
Skip quickly and lightly through the spaces. Pause to reach forwards with an arm slowly and strongly as if to pick a banana from a large bunch.
The biggest, best banana is right in the middle of the bunch. Can it be reached?
Skip and pause to reach strongly and slowly, forwards or sideways, to finish in a stretched shape on one foot.

109

The mini-beast entertainers

Age range
Three to nine.

Emphasis
Action and speed.

Daring daddy-long-legs.
Make wide, stretched shapes on hands and feet, then step into a variety of balanced shapes, ie on one arm and one leg; one leg only; on both arms and one leg with one leg stretched in the air, and on two legs with one or both arms stretched.

The snail race.
Form pairs and curl up on the floor side by side, slowly pulling along with arched backs and elbows and knees on the floor.

The grasshopper's long jump.
Take long leaps, feet together, from a crouched position. Hands must touch the floor at the end of each jump.

The air display.
Whirl and swoop around the room high and low,
opening and closing 'wings', 'hovering' and 'buzzing'.

The spider on the high wire.
Spin slowly and step along a straight pathway into
another space with arms outstretched as though
balancing. Exaggerate the movements to show off the
spider's amazing agility.

Big Boots the terrific, tap-dancing beetle!
Move spontaneously with rhythmic, tapping feet to a
given beat on the spot, forwards, backwards, sideways
and with a partner.

Flit the fearless fly!
Walk on hands and feet with heads leading, or with
chests facing the ceiling. Change direction from
forwards to backwards to sideways.

   Put hoops on the floor to represent sticky cakes. Ask
the 'flies' to tiptoe around the edge, then jump in and out
of them at a given signal. The 'flies' then pull and push
their way upwards and outwards.

Parading and performing.
Allow a free choice of one of the mini-beasts and
develop activities alone in pairs, in threes or in groups.

Out and about

In this chapter, links are made between home, school and journeys. The children are stimulated into creative movement through their everyday experiences of crowds, supermarkets, trains and stations. The humour of these activities will appeal to teachers and children alike.

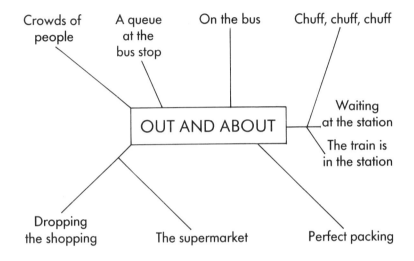

Crowds of people

'People here, people there;
People, people, everywhere.
Rushing here, dashing there,
Never time to stop and stare.'

Kate Harrison

Age range
Six to eleven.

Emphasis
Travelling and stopping.

People here, people there;
Sprint along winding pathways, stopping sometimes in statue shapes.
People, people, everywhere. Where are my friends?
Dash quickly along twisting pathways, pausing sometimes in high, stretched balancing shapes on one or both feet, looking over the tops of each other's heads.
Rushing here, dashing there; are they here?
Run quickly and lightly, sometimes pausing to crouch or lie down to look along the floor.
Are they there?
Run quickly and lightly, sometimes pausing to wave to someone at the other end of the room.
Never time to stop and stare.
Step slowly into a space, then stop and stare straight ahead. Turn to face a new direction and run into another space.

Further challenges can be created for older children by allowing free choice on each statue stop, for example balancing looking over tops of heads; crouching or lying down on the floor; or standing still and waving to someone on the other side of the room.

A queue at the bus stop

Age range
Eight to eleven.

Emphasis
Under, over and around.

Someone at the back of the queue is desperate to find a way of getting to the front. The person at the front of the queue ties a shoe lace or drops some money. The person at the back uses the opportunity to get to the front.
Work in pairs, one behind the other. The front person bends down to a crouched position. The second person steps quickly or jumps over the person in front.
Where is the bus? The front person looks over imaginary vehicle tops or flags down the bus. The person at the back uses the opportunity to jump the queue.

The front person stands on tiptoe with legs wide apart or stretching into a side balance. The back person quickly crawls or rolls underneath.
The person at the front of the queue is distracted, listening to their personal stereo. What a good track! The person behind moves to the front of the queue.
The front person bounces up and down, clutching imaginary headphones. The back person creeps slowly and carefully round to the front.
A terrible time at the bus stop.
Join together to form groups of four and stand one behind the other. Use the above ideas to form a sequence which can be repeated as each person reaches the head of the queue.

On the bus

Age range
Four to seven.

Emphasis
Quickly changing from one action to another.

'Hold on tight!' **Oh dear, we're not quite tall enough to reach the bar.**
Make big bouncing jumps on the spot, feet together, with one arm reaching up high, legs stretched then bent at the knees.
'Fares please!' Where have I put my money?
Stand on one spot, slapping hands against body, high and low.

'Room on top!' Going up the spiral staircase with heavy shopping.
Take slow heavy steps, body bent over, along a circular pathway.
The bus game.
Form groups of three. One person calls the conductor's commands, the others react with the appropriate action which must be continued until the command changes. Repeat until each child has had a turn at calling commands.

Chuff, chuff, chuff

Age range
Three to seven.

Emphasis
Basic spacing skills as an individual and in group lines.

Here comes the train, chugging down the line.
Take strong, rhythmic steps from space to space, with arms moving in small, strong circles.
Here is the station – open all the doors!
Take strong, rhythmic steps from space to space, sometimes stopping, one arm 'opening' strongly forwards and around to the side, reversing to 'close the door'.
There's a hill up ahead.
Take strong, slow, rhythmic steps from space to space, arms moving in slow, strong, small circles.

Chugging backwards into the siding.
Step slowly, strongly and carefully backwards, circling arms and looking over shoulders.

Join up the carriages.
Start in spaces, with one child as leader or driver. The 'driver' chugs in and out of the spaces and gently taps 'carriages' while passing by. The 'carriages' join up by placing hands on the shoulders of the 'carriage' in front. The 'driver' leads the train around the room, forwards, backwards or into the station to open the doors.

Racing down the track on the other side.
Take strong, fast, rhythmic steps from space to space, arms moving in fast circles.

Up we go, over the hump-back bridge.
Step on tiptoes with legs straight, arms circling.

Down, down, through the deep dark tunnel.
Step with bent knees, crouching low, arms circling.

Clickety-clack, over the points.
Take fast, tottering steps from space to space, rocking the upper body from side to side and circling arms quickly and jerkily.

Waiting at the station

Age range
Five to eleven.

Emphasis
Movement in, out, around, over and between.

Rows and rows of bags and cases. Waiting is boring. Let's make up a dance with the bags and cases.
Work with a partner or in small groups and make up a dance using some of the following movements:

- Running, skipping or hopping in and out of the bags and cases, forwards and backwards.
- Running, skipping or hopping around a bag or a case, forwards and backwards, quickly and lightly.
- Jumping high over a bag or case, forwards or backwards, in a curled shape, a flat shape, or turning.
- Leaping over one bag after another.
- Starting next to a bag or case, lifting one leg over it while turning on one foot.
- Making a simple stepping pattern to travel from one bag or case to another, using forwards, backwards, sideways and turning steps.

Perfect packing

Age range
Six to eleven.

Emphasis
Isolating body parts.

Trying to shut the suitcase.
Push with flat hands, slowly and strongly, towards the floor.

Oh well, maybe we shouldn't have packed the seven towels!
Push slowly and strongly, starting with hands high above the head, finishing with hands on the floor.
. . . or the six pairs of trainers!
Push slowly and strongly with other body parts – hips, back, legs.
. . . or the five sweat-shirts!
Push slowly and strongly towards a partner with hands, back, hips or feet.

. . . or the four hats, or the three pairs of sunglasses!
Squeeze slowly and strongly with knees, as if holding the suitcase between them.
. . . or the two beach umbrellas!
Stamp quickly and strongly with one foot and then the other.
. . . or the deck-chair!
Jump quickly and powerfully with knees high, landing on both feet, crouched near the floor.

Let's take nothing at all!
Finish with one huge jump, flinging the arms high in the air, landing on both feet and then sitting or flopping on the floor.

The train is in the station

Age range
Three to eleven.

Emphasis
Groups working in circles and lines.

Loading luggage.
Form a circle or line, holding hands, arms outstretched. Drop the arms and keep this distance between each person, without touching each other. Then, using real or imaginary bags and cases, stretch slowly and strongly sideways to take a bag. Next, stretch slowly and strongly to the other side to give it to the next person; or stretch slowly and strongly, forwards or backwards, to take the bag, passing it high over the head to give it to the next person; or stretch slowly and strongly through the legs to take from or give to the next person.

Performing porters.
Pass bags or cases, slowly and carefully, from one person to another, forwards, backwards, sideways, over or under, without using the hands, for example: lifting

with the knees, turning on the bottom, sliding with a foot, carrying on the back, balancing on the chest.
Groovy guards.
Mix up all the above actions, using as much variety as possible.

Terrible timing.
Continue as above, gradually getting faster and faster.
Perhaps everyone and everything ends up in a heap.
**Oh dear! All that fuss and now we've missed the train.
We'll have to wait for the next one!**

The supermarket

Age range
Three to eight.

Emphasis
Going and stopping in contrasting body shapes.

Up, down and across the aisles, searching for this week's special offer.
Hold arms out in front and clench fists as if steering a supermarket trolley. Walk strongly and purposefully, sometimes forwards, sometimes backwards, sometimes fast and sometimes slowly, changing direction at right angles sharply or leading or following a partner. **Why is it that whatever we want is on the top shelf?** Pause to make a strong stretched shape, or jump quickly, reaching high before continuing to travel.

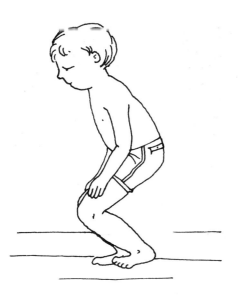

Dropping the shopping

Age range
Three to eleven.

Emphasis
Changing shapes and sizes.

The shopping bag smashes on the pavement. The can of syrup dents.
Start from a straight standing position, then sharply change shape by quickly bending the back. Change from dented shape to shape by quickly bending different joints – elbows, knees, ankles, neck, wrists, shoulders.

Or hidden underneath the bottom shelf?
Pause to crouch quickly or lie flat on the floor before continuing to travel.
Or at the bottom of the freezer?
Stand with straight legs, slowly reaching forwards and down towards the floor; reaching sideways and down towards the floor; reaching slowly and strongly, forwards and down or sideways and down over a partner's arms or back.

The lid's come off – out oozes the syrup.
Start from a tall, stretched shape, then slowly and smoothly sink to the floor, one body part at a time. Then slowly and smoothly roll and spread along the floor into a wide, flat shape.
Out fall the pasta twists.
Turn quickly from place to place, pausing in a twisted shape before turning quickly to another place.
Squirt goes the washing-up liquid.
Starting from a crouched position, make fast, powerful jumps in long, straight, stretched shapes, forwards, backwards, sideways and round.
Foamy bubbles fall.
Slowly and gently sink and settle near the floor.
Cream cakes squelch and squash.
Stand side by side with a partner, starting in stretched shapes, and slowly and strongly turn towards each other, then slowly and strongly twist around each other and finally slowly sink together side by side, or one on top of the other, on to the floor.

Acknowledgements

The poem 'Go Wind' on page 18 is reprinted with permission of Atheneum Publishers, an imprint of Macmillan Publishing Company, from *I Feel The Same Way* by Lilian Moore. Copyright © 1967 by Lilian Moore.

The activities 'Meg the witch', 'Mog the magic cat', 'Owl' and 'Meg's eggs' were inspired by the *Meg and Mog* books by Helen Nicoll and Jan Pienkowski (published by Heinemann and Penguin).

Some of the activities in this book were originally published in *Child Education, Infant Projects* and *Junior Projects* magazines (Scholastic Publications).

Other Scholastic books

Bright Ideas

The *Bright Ideas* books provide a wealth of resources for busy primary school teachers. There are now more than 20 titles published, providing clearly explained and illustrated ideas on topics ranging from *Spelling* and *Maths Games* to *World of Work* and *Using Books in the Classroom*. Each book contains material which can be photocopied for use in the classroom.

Teacher Handbooks

The *Teacher Handbooks* give an overview of the latest research in primary education, and show how it can be put into practice in the classroom. Covering all the core areas of the curriculum, the *Teacher Handbooks* are indispensable to the new teacher as a source of information and useful to the experienced teacher as a quick reference guide.

Management Books

The *Management Books* are designed to help teachers to organise their time, classroom and teaching more efficiently. The books deal with topical issues, such as *Parents and Schools* and organising and planning *Project Teaching*, and are written by authors with lots of practical advice and experiences to share.

Let's Investigate

Let's Investigate is an exciting range of photocopiable maths activity books giving open-ended investigative tasks. The series will complement and extend any existing maths programme. Designed to cover the 6 to 12-year-old age range these books are ideal for small group or individual work. Each book presents progressively more difficult concepts and many of the activities can be adapted for use throughout the primary school. Detailed teacher's notes outlining the objectives of each photocopiable sheet and suggesting follow-up activities have been included.